Health and My Body

Care for Your Teeth

by Martha E. H. Rustad

PEBBLE
a capstone imprint

Pebble Explore is published by Pebble, an imprint of Capstone.
1710 Roe Crest Drive
North Mankato, Minnesota 56003
www.capstonepub.com

**Library of Congress Cataloging-in-Publication Data is available on
the Library of Congress website.**
ISBN: 978-1-9771-2388-6 (library binding)
ISBN: 978-1-9771-2688-7 (paperback)
ISBN: 978-1-9771-2425-8 (eBook PDF)
Summary: Good dental hygiene is important. Learn good habits for
healthy teeth.

Image Credits
Getty Images: Tom Stewart, 23; iStockphoto: hocus-focus, 27, Yarinca,
16; Shutterstock: Alila Medical Media, 7, Dream79, 18, Everything is
stock, 20, Gelpi, 9, Ilya Andriyanov, 6, Littlekidmoment, Cover, Monkey
Business Images, 5, 24, 28, photonova, design element throughout,
Rido, 29, Rob Marmion, 15, Robert Kneschke, 19, Santhosh Varghese,
8, snapgalleria, 11, TairA, 4, Tefi, 21, Vanatchanan, 12

Editorial Credits
Editor: Michelle Parkin; Designer: Sarah Bennett; Media Researcher:
Morgan Walters; Production Specialist: Laura Manthe

All internet sites appearing in back matter were available and
accurate when this book was sent to press.

Printed in the United States   5619

Table of Contents

Bold words are in the glossary.

Your Teeth Are Important!

Bite an apple. Talk to a friend. Smile for a picture. What helps you do all of these things? Your teeth!

You use your teeth every day. You couldn't chew your food without them. Teeth help you form words. They help you make certain sounds. You show your teeth when you smile. Let's find out how to take care of your teeth.

What Are Teeth?

Teeth are hard and white. The top part of the tooth is called the crown. This is the part you can see. **Gums** line the bottom of your teeth. They cover the roots.

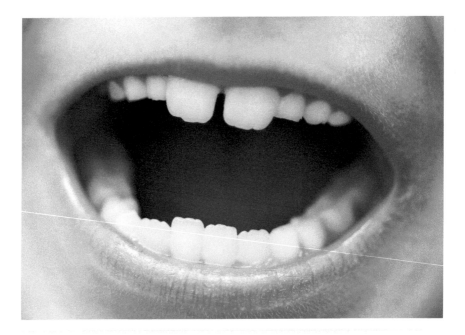

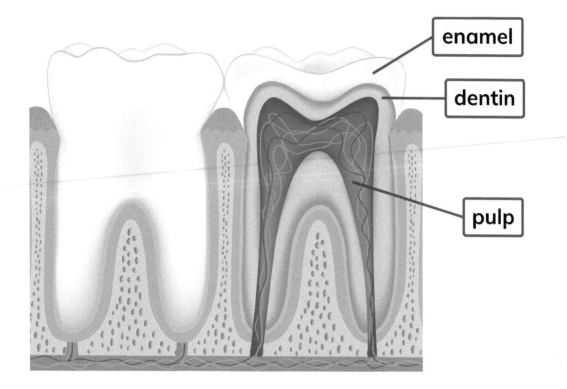

enamel

dentin

pulp

A tooth has three layers. The outside layer is called the enamel. It is hard and shiny. Dentin is the middle layer. It is not as hard as the enamel. Dentin protects the inside layer, called the pulp. The pulp is the softest layer.

You will have two sets of teeth in your life. The first set is your baby teeth. You will have 20 baby teeth. These teeth start to fall out around age 5.

Have you lost a tooth? A baby tooth feels wiggly before it falls out. A missing tooth can change your smile. You may sound differently when you talk. But don't worry. A new, permanent tooth will grow in its place. Permanent teeth are bigger than baby teeth. You will have 32 permanent teeth.

Look at your teeth in a mirror. They come in different shapes. Each type of tooth has a job to do.

Your front teeth are called incisors. There are four incisors on the top of your mouth. Four more line the bottom. Incisors help you bite food into pieces.

Your canine teeth are next to your incisors. You have four canine teeth. These sharp, pointed teeth help you hold and tear food.

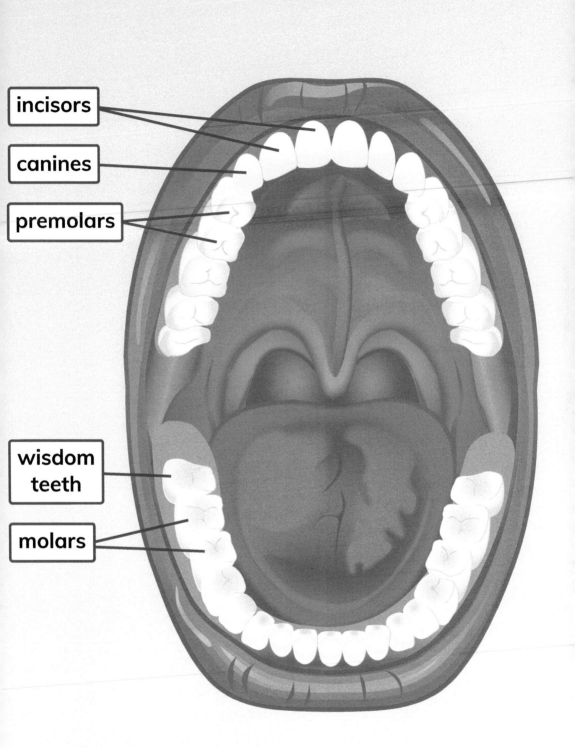

incisors

canines

premolars

wisdom
teeth

molars

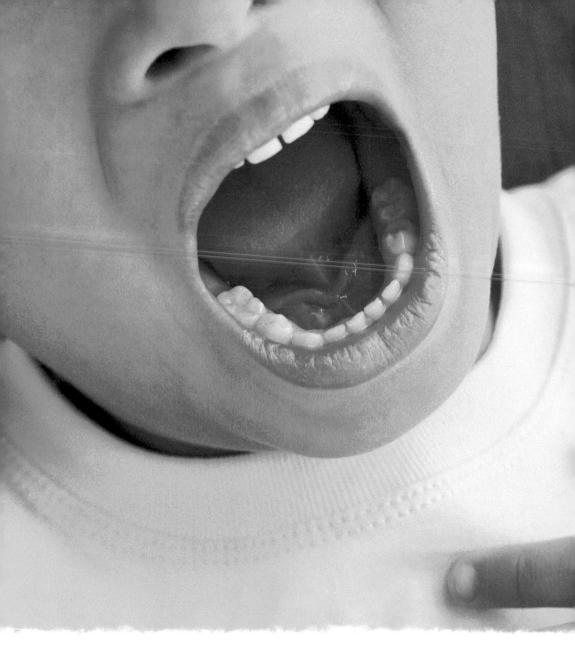

Premolars are near the back of your
mouth. These teeth are bumpy on top.
They help you chew and grind food.

Molars are in the very back of your mouth. You will have four molars by the time you are 6 years old. Four more molars will come in around age 12. Molars are your strongest teeth. They grind food before you swallow it.

The last teeth to come in are called wisdom teeth. These molars come in around age 20.

Taking Care of Your Teeth

You need the right tools to take care of your teeth. Use a soft toothbrush that won't scratch your gums. Use a toothpaste with **fluoride**. This helps keep your teeth strong.

Brush your teeth two times every day. Brush after you eat breakfast. Brush again before you go to bed. You should brush in a circle on the front, back, and top of each tooth. Brush your teeth for two minutes. No timer? Sing "Twinkle Twinkle Little Star" in your head four times.

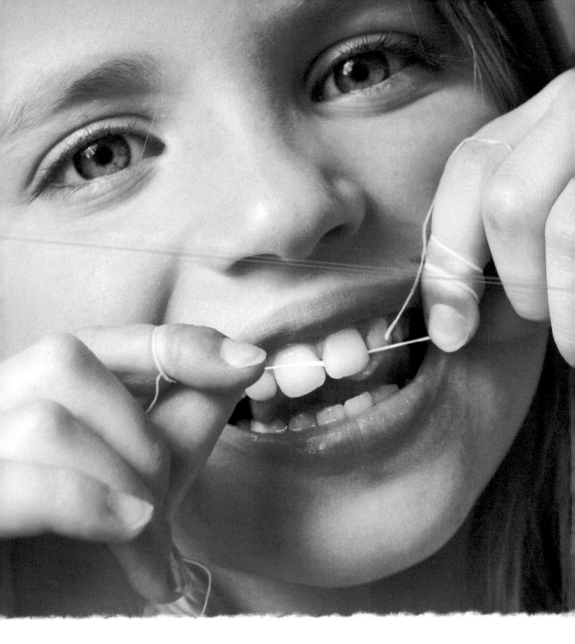

Use floss once a day. Floss is a kind of string covered with wax. It slips between your teeth. Floss can loosen food stuck between your teeth.

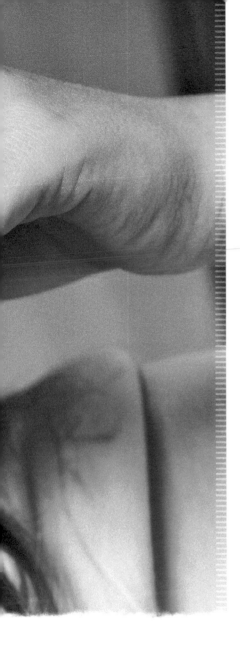

How do you use floss? Take a long string of floss from the roll. Wrap most of it around your middle or index fingers. The floss should be tight! Move the string back and forth between each tooth.

Eating healthy food keeps your teeth strong. Apples, carrots, and other crunchy fruits and vegetables scrape **plaque** off teeth. Eggs, milk, and cheese keep teeth strong and healthy. Nuts and seeds have oils that help the outer layer of your teeth.

Drink water. Soda, juice, and other sweet drinks aren't good for your teeth. They have lots of sugar. Sugar makes acids that hurt teeth and gums.

Chewy candies can stick to teeth. After a while, they can break down tooth enamel.

What's a Cavity?

Have you ever had a toothache? It hurts! That pain may be from a **cavity**. A cavity is a tiny hole in the tooth. Over time, the hole can get bigger. It can go deeper into the tooth. Ouch!

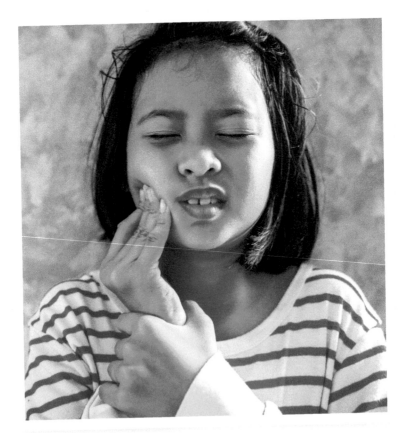

A cavity is caused by plaque. Plaque is slimy and yellow. It is made up of germs that hurt your teeth. When plaque sticks to your teeth, it wears away the enamel. If you think you have a cavity, it's important to see a **dentist**. He or she can help.

healthy tooth   tooth with plaque

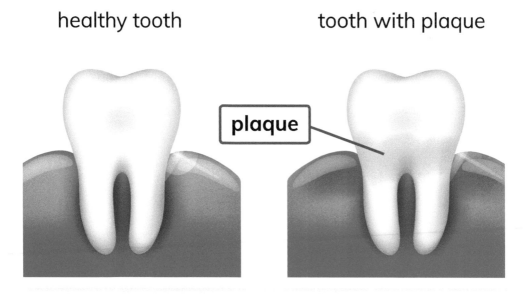

plaque

A Visit to the Dentist

Go to a dentist's office two times a year. Dental **hygienists** work at the dentist's office. They clean and **polish** your teeth. The hygienist will check to make sure you are brushing and using floss. He or she will look at your gums. The hygienist may even put a fluoride gel on your teeth. This can fix tiny holes in your enamel.

X-rays of your teeth and jaw may be taken. An X-ray can show cavities hidden between your teeth or problems under your gums.

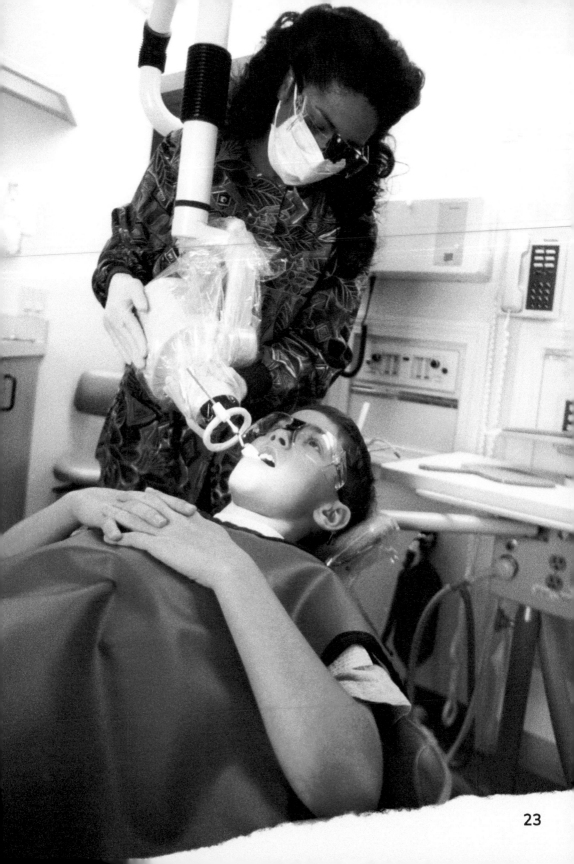

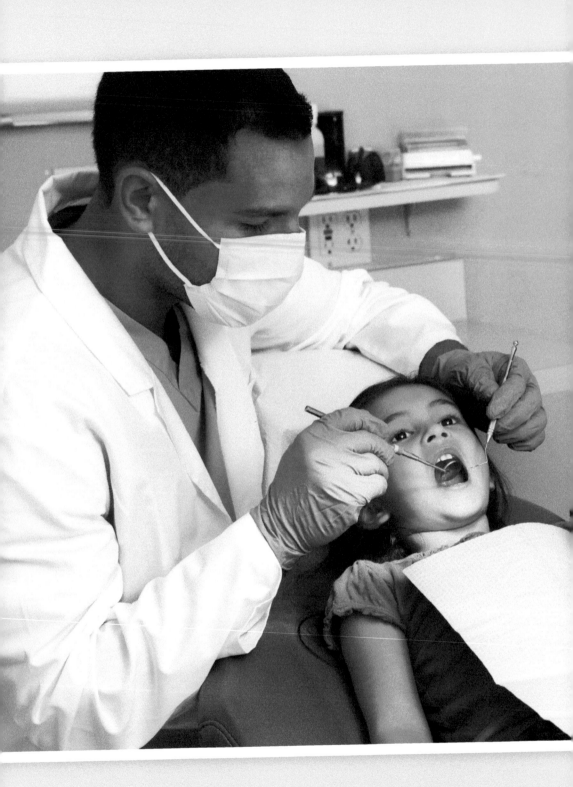

After your cleaning, the dentist will look at your teeth. He or she will study your X-rays. The dentist will look closely for cavities.

Dentists may put a **sealant** on your teeth. A sealant is a thin coating. It is painted on your back teeth. This protects the enamel. Dentists put sealants on both baby and permanent teeth.

Tooth Troubles

Your teeth are strong. But bumps, hits, and falls can cause teeth to chip, break, or even fall out. If a permanent tooth falls out, a new tooth will not grow back. Dentists can fix broken and chipped teeth.

Your teeth may be crooked. Your upper and lower jaws may not be the same size. Your dentist may tell you to see an **orthodontist**. This doctor can put braces on your teeth. Over time, the braces help straighten your teeth.

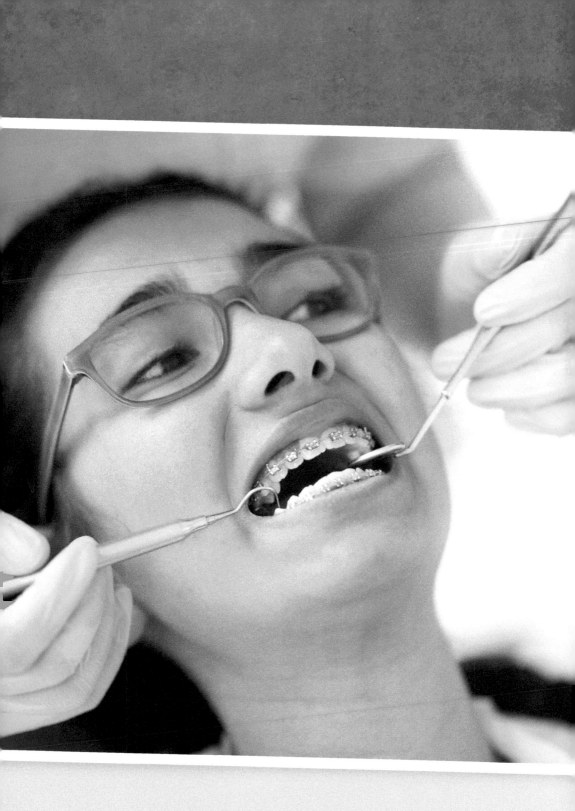

It takes a whole team of people to keep your teeth healthy. But you are in charge of your mouth. It's up to you to brush and use floss every day.

Take care of your teeth. They will help you eat, talk, and smile for years to come!

Glossary

cavity (KAH-vuh-tee)—a hole in a tooth caused by decay, or rotting

dentist (DEN-tist)—a person who is trained to check, clean, and fix teeth

fluoride (FLOOR-yd)—a natural mineral put on teeth to make them stronger and prevent cavities

gum (GUHM)—the firm flesh around the base of a person's tooth

hygienist (hye-JEN-ist)—person who is trained to help the dentist; hygienists clean teeth and take X-rays

orthodontist (or-thuh-DON-tist)—a specialist who straightens uneven teeth

plaque (PLAK)—the coating of food, saliva, and bacteria that forms on teeth and can cause rotting

polish (POL-ish)—to rub something to make it shine

sealant (SEEL-uhnt)—thin, plastic coating painted on chewing surfaces of back teeth to prevent decay

X-ray (EKS-ray)—a picture of the inside of the tooth

Read More

Arnex, Lynda. We Stay Clean. New York: Gareth Stevens Publishing, 2020.

Marsico, Katie. Brush Your Teeth! Ann Arbor, MI: Cherry Lake Publishing, 2019.

Mason, David I. A. Brush Your Grizzly Bear Grin. Minneapolis: Cantata Learning, 2016.

Internet Sites

American Dental Association, Toothbrushing Tunes Kids (and Parents) Will Love
https://www.mouthhealthy.org/en/kids-brushing-playlist

Cool Kid Facts, Teeth Facts
https://www.coolkidfacts.com/teeth-facts/

Kids Health, Your Teeth
https://kidshealth.org/en/kids/teeth.html

Index